Copyright © 2008 by Dr. Travis Bradberry. All rights
reserved. Printed in the United States of America. No part of
this book may be used or reproduced in any manner whatsoever
without written permission except in the case of brief quotations
embodied in critical articles and reviews.

FIRST EDITION

Designed by William Ruoto

Library of Congress Cataloging-in-Publication Data has been
applied for.

To all of us, for those moments when we find ourselves swooping in on a problem, squawking up a storm, and flapping our wings about, only to discover that we have just pooped all over everything. . .

Contents

Contents

The Model

Part One

The Fable

Chapter

1

The Seagull Manager

FOR AS LONG AS HE could remember, Charlie had been flying high at work. When he shared this sentiment with others, most forgave the pun—not just because Charlie was a seagull, but, quite simply, because he was a seagull who truly loved his job. And up until recently, it was an easy job to love. As the head gull in a flock whose sole undertaking was pillaging the food court of a marine theme park in Southern California, he felt business was a genuine pleasure.

Many years earlier, Charlie's flock had lived with the rest of their breed at the seashore. Charlie was well known among the gulls because he was gutsy and passionate, and his head was always swimming with ideas. One day he shared a fascinating vision of a place where a little ingenuity would ensure their prosperity. Charlie had seen the place first hand, and many of the gulls returned day after day to hear him talk about it. In time, the cocksure leader convinced a group of them to break away from the petty, pecking grind at the seashore and join him to form their own flock in a place they knew only as the food court.

When the new flock landed at the marine park, they found the food court was even better than they had imagined. All of the food there was fattening and easy to come by; the unsuspecting humans were no match for the gulls' aggressive dive-bombing. For years the resourceful gulls enjoyed a life of abundance, snatching food from unsuspecting tourists by day and roosting safely on a craggy hillside at night. While the other flocks back at the seashore battled the pelicans and humans for the ocean's dwindling supply of clever, speedy fish, Charlie's flock enjoyed a generous supply of tasty grub brought to them daily by the patrons of the food court.

And no gull in the flock knew more than Charlie about when, where, and how a gull could nab a hearty meal. Charlie was so good at eating that the flock named him their manager. Not that there was much for him to manage. There was so much food around that keeping the flock content and their bellies full was easy. For the longest time, Charlie didn't have to worry much about keeping everyone happy.

Nowadays, things were decidedly different.

At first, there was the odd baby pecking out of an egg here and there, but the babies grew quickly. Soon, the newest members of the flock had hatchlings of their own. In what felt like no time at all, the flock's size tripled. Unfortunately, the food court did not.

The marine park continued to be a popular place, but only so many sunburned tourists could squeeze into the food court at one time. Initially, the flock's new mouths to feed were welcomed with open wings because there was plenty of food to go around, but it was only a matter of time before abundance and prosperity gave way to bickering over who got to peck first at an abandoned plate of nachos.

In the old days, a squabble among flock members wouldn't last long—some of the birds would simply move on to the next ready meal. As time and change transformed food into a scarce commodity, the squabbles became more frequent and more dramatic. With each passing month, the food supply became increasingly inadequate, and the gulls' hunger eroded the camaraderie of the team.

When the latest hatchlings reached maturity, Charlie still felt he was doing an excellent job running the show. He filled his days with the same essential activities he always had—negotiating the boundaries of marine park turf with other birds, resolving conflicts between flock members, undertaking an occasional grunt mission to dive-bomb unsuspecting children and snatch their sweets, and (for stress relief) dropping precision-guided munitions down the backs of shirtless sightseers. It was business as usual for Charlie, and he loved it.

Squawk!

That is, until he returned to roost one blustery evening and found the flock in the middle of a heated discussion. Charlie overheard small snippets of their conversation—something to do with concerns about the food supply—and he immediately mistook their debate for bickering. As he was prone to do, Charlie was squawking orders before his feet even touched the ground. He landed in the middle of the flock, flapped his wings like crazy to back them off, and finished with a tirade that supposedly held the best course of action.

Usually, when Charlie finished "solving" the problem, he would fly off to his next responsibility, leaving little opportunity for discussion. But on this night, with all the gulls gathered together in the roost, he had nowhere else to go. Charlie's slow realization of this fact created an awkward silence. He strutted around with his chest puffed out and wings pulled back long after he had run out of things to say. He looked at the faces surrounding him and realized they didn't hold the usual array of befuddled looks. Instead, the gulls looked strangely determined, almost as if they were expecting this.

Scott stepped forward. He was the flock's top performer, and his glossy coat of feathers and stout frame were a stark contrast to the emaciated gulls behind him. Scott had been with the flock since the beginning, and he was not one to mince words, "Charlie, we've got a serious problem here."

"Really? What's the matter?" Charlie asked, assuming there had been some type of accident.

"We're hungry, Charlie. Nobody's getting fed," Scott replied, glancing at the gaunt birds huddled on either side of him.

Charlie scanned the flock of gaunt seagulls himself. "Oh, man, just look at all of you! Are those dang sparrows snatching all of our food?" he asked. The flock responded with a profound silence. "Are you listening to me?" Charlie demanded. "Don't worry—you don't need to worry— just get to it. You guys can outwit any bird that's leaving you hungry. I know it."

"Charlie, you're not getting it," Maya said as she squeezed her way forward. "That bird—the one that's leaving us hungry—it's you." Like Scott, Maya had been with the flock since its inception, and her wisdom and insight were highly regarded. Unlike Scott, she was generally understated, and her poignant allegation sent an immediate murmur through the flock.

"Whoa? *What*? *Me?*" Charlie stuttered, dumbfounded. "I'm not the one who's been eating all of your food. I hardly even see all of you most days."

"Well, that's part of the problem, Charlie," Maya said.

"What do you mean, exactly? How am *I* eating *your* food if I'm not even here?" Charlie scratched his head with the tip of his wing as he spoke.

Scott stepped back in, "You're not literally eating our food, Charlie. The problem is we don't have enough food to go around, and under your leadership things aren't getting any better."

"How am I supposed to make sure everyone has enough to eat when you don't even tell me there's not enough food to go around?" Charlie asked indignantly.

"We've been trying to tell you for some time, actually, but you just don't listen to us. Kind of like tonight—you assume you know what's going on. It's why we gathered here, so we can talk to you about it."

"All right, if that's the way it is, then let's hear what I'm doing wrong," Charlie continued. "I want to know how *I'm* responsible for *you all* not getting enough to eat."

Yufan, a recent import from Taiwan who had joined the flock (he'd become trapped in a shipping container that was, fortunately for him, filled with cans of tuna, although his beak was still a little dull from the journey), stepped forward and asked if he could share the flock's example with Charlie. Heads nodded enthusiastically around the semicircle. As Yufan prepared to speak, Charlie felt a lump growing in his throat. *Everyone is in on this one,* he thought.

"Charlie, you don't understand the problems we're having with the food supply because you aren't around most of the time. You disappear until you see us squabbling or we ask for your help, and then you come swooping in out of nowhere and . . ."

"Well, I'm busy. Would you rather I followed you around all day and fed you myself?" Charlie asked sarcastically.

There was a nervous shuffling of webbed feet until Scott ventured, "Now, come on, Charlie, that's not fair, and it's not even the point. Please allow Yufan to finish."

Charlie held out the tips of his wings toward the group, took a couple of steps backward, lowered his head, and pursed his beak together tightly to let everyone know that he would now keep it shut and hear them out.

"When you swoop in on us because we're having a problem with something," Yufan continued, "you don't get the full story because you don't even try. You're too busy squawking to listen."

Scott joined in again. "Just like tonight. You go right into telling us what to do like it's all so simple and we're too stupid to know what to do."

"Wait just a minute!" Charlie spat. "I *never* called anyone stupid."

Although some of the flock began to cower, Scott wasn't fazed. He knew Charlie well and had thought it would come to this. "You're right, Charlie, you didn't. But it sure feels like you think we're stupid when you swoop in out of nowhere and fire a bunch of orders at us like we're a bunch of hatchlings that can't come up with any worthwhile ideas on our own. And what's worse is that you take off and leave us behind to clean up your mess." Scott was on a roll and felt that he just might be getting through to his seagull manager, "It's like the time—"

"Like when?" Charlie was through with listening and back to butting in.

Yufan jumped in. "All right, Charlie, I know what he was going to say. He's talking about last Thursday afternoon. Everybody remember that fat, hairy guy in the orange tank top who bought his wife a super-sized plate of nachos with jalapeños right before the food court closed? The humans started to argue—something about she's allergic to jalapeños and he should've known better—and then the two of them stormed off and left the nachos right there on the table."

"And?" Like most who are forced to endure a heap of criticism, Charlie was growing more impatient by the minute.

"And we all flew over there for the feast. But even with that huge plate of nachos, there wasn't enough room for every gull to get his beak in there. So, we had to stop eating and figure out what to do."

"Yes, and . . ." Charlie beckoned, tapping his foot.

"And we weren't sure what to do. There wasn't enough for everyone, and there wasn't any other food available, so we couldn't just send some of the flock off to another table. Plus, no one really had any kind of priority on the nachos 'cause that couple just left them there." Yufan finally had Charlie's attention. "We're finding ourselves in situations like these every day lately. That's why so many of us are going hungry."

Charlie had calmed down considerably, "All right,

I see your point. That situation poses an interesting dilemma. But I still don't see what this has to do with my management."

"You don't?" Maya blurted out in genuine amazement.

"No, I don't. Is there some kind of connection between me and your problem last Thursday?" Charlie asked.

Yufan shook his head with disappointment. Behind him, all the exasperated gulls rolled their eyes.

Naturally, Scott took over. "Well, Charlie, Maya went off and found you so you could help us figure out what to do with those nachos. You swooped in, landed in the middle of the table, and shot off a bunch of orders that didn't do us any good. You said something glib, like 'Whoever snatched these nachos gets to eat them, and the rest of you need to go find your own food. There isn't enough for everybody.' And then you grabbed a couple for yourself and were gone. Poof! It should've been problem solved, but instead you left us right where we were before, minus some nachos."

"It also made me feel like a foolish hatchling—and look like one to everyone else—when you told the flock that I shouldn't have come to get you and we should be able to figure these things out on our own," Maya said. "We'd been sizing up our options for some time and were planning on sharing our ideas and potential strategies with you. But when you got there, you didn't even give them any consideration. You left us worse off than we were before."

"Ya, instead of helping us solve the problem, it was like you, well, like you . . ." one of the gulls in the back said, his voice trailing off nervously.

"Like I what?" Charlie barked.

"Like you pooped all over everything," Scott piped up reluctantly.

An almost audible hush fell over the flock.

Swallowing hard, Maya decided to back Scott and drive the point home, "You pooped all over us and *our* problem—you pooped on our ideas, you pooped on our hard work, and then you just flew off and left us there to clean up the mess. To clean up *your* mess."

Charlie felt as if he'd just taken a crushing physical blow. Seagulls pooped on people intentionally to demonstrate their superiority. It was unthinkable that one gull would ever do such a thing to another gull.

Charlie's body began to feel heavy as he stood there, motionless, in the midst of the deafening silence. The sting of his flock's feedback made it hard to think straight. He was failing them, and he didn't know what to do. Finally, with all eyes still fixed intently upon him, Charlie spoke, "OK. I see how it is. You've made your point loud and clear. I'm outta here."

And with those words, Charlie flew away.

Chapter 2

A Chance Encounter

AFTER CHARLIE LEFT THAT NIGHT, the flock continued meeting to explore options for finding food. Finding a new manager seemed like an obvious solution, but no one in the flock was the right fit. Maya had great ideas, but she shuddered to think of herself at the center of the flock's attention. The flock considered Scott a leader of sorts, but he knew that his brazen and blunt style of interacting with others would cause too many problems. Yufan seemed like the best candidate. He was a hard worker and a social butterfly, but he was perfectly happy with his position and had no interest in managing seagulls. The flock decided that Charlie was just going to have to change.

Charlie returned to the roost early the following morning with his tail feathers between his legs. He was relieved to discover that the other gulls still wanted him there. Scott was eager to discuss the previous evening's events. While the rest of the flock took off to the food court to begin the workday, Scott and Charlie stepped aside for a chat.

"I just want you to know that we hadn't figured on having our feedback land so harshly on your shoulders, Charlie," Scott explained.

Charlie nodded as if a truce had been struck.

"But I also want you to accept that our concerns are real. I mean, just look at us." Scott paused to observe the cadre of seagulls that were waddling, fluttering, and flying their way toward the food court. "We've grown and changed a lot since we first came here. The old ways just don't seem to be cutting it anymore. We're stuck Charlie. We need your guidance, your collaboration, your support, even, to help us get through this. Every gull deserves a full belly. After all, isn't that why we followed you here in the first place?"

Having had an evening to calm down and think through the gravity of the situation, Charlie was more open to the flock's feedback than he had been the night before. "You guys are right," he admitted. "I just want you to know that I *have* been trying. I just didn't realize that I wasn't doing a very good job. I'll do everything in my power to fix this. I'm willing to change."

News of Charlie's desire to turn over a new leaf was well received by the rest of the flock. The gulls had newfound energy to put back into their work—until the weeks flew by and nothing happened. Sure, Charlie was a little more patient with the flock when they squabbled over food or asked for help, but it remained apparent that he didn't think there were enough hours in the day for *him* to solve *their* problems. So, the flock decided to present their own ideas for how to handle the increasingly desperate situation.

The flock had always talked about how much food must be in the park, if they could just figure out how to get their beaks on it. Surely their tried-and-true strategy of snagging food from inattentive diners couldn't be the only way to keep their bellies firm and round.

Scott was more brazen and prone to taking risks than the average gull, and he had been with the flock since they first came to the food court. It was natural for him to suggest that they quit lamenting the food they were missing out on and go straight to the source. He'd noticed that all of the food served by the food court was delivered early each morning before the sun came up. If some members of the flock just got up earlier, they could probably snag enough food from the delivery men to feed the entire flock all day.

Much to everyone's surprise, Charlie heard Scott's idea out and even acknowledged its potential, but he wasn't about to let the flock implement the strategy. "There's no way we're adding a night shift," Charlie told them. "It will be a major disruption to our schedule. We can't have a bunch of tired zombies roaming the food court.

This flock feeds at the food court—*during the day*—in one shift. Period."

Maya's idea was next. Her clever strategy was focused on another untapped source of food in the park—the gift shops. She noticed that most of the park's gift shops had shelves filled with snacks and candy to prop open their doors and catch the eye of hungry customers. Maya wondered why a stealthy gull couldn't just wait until the clerk was preoccupied, swoop on in, and fly off with a tasty bag of chips.

Charlie could sense the flock's growing furor over his rejection of Scott's idea, so he decided to let Maya give hers a try. Charlie understood that Maya's strategy was something of a stealth mission, so he let her be the guinea pig. Just as she often was with her peers, Maya was quiet as a feather on her way into the store. The initial missions went beautifully, and she returned with a bag of chips every time.

News of Maya's successful runs convinced Scott that he should give it a go himself. The flock knew Scott had trouble keeping his beak shut, so they reminded him to approach the store quietly, but Scott was too enamored with visions of heroic commando missions that would save the flock to heed their request. He waited outside the store until he found his moment, went in squawking, and came skidding out on his rear with the assistance of the clerk's broom. Charlie promptly announced that stealth missions did not work and that no further raids on the park's gift shops would be conducted.

Yufan's idea was the last one for Charlie to ruin. Everyone feared it was the last thing standing between an easy life in the food court and a return to the miserable seashore.

Yufan was something of a bulldozer when it came to getting work done. No matter how daunting the challenge, he was the first gull to spread his wings and get to work, not stopping until he was done. Sleeping, eating, and free time meant little to Yufan when there was an unfinished project at hand. It was only natural that Yufan's idea was something of a sink-or-swim proposition. His system was simple: find enough to eat and you get to stay; have trouble feeding yourself and you're back to the seashore.

Naturally, Charlie loved the idea. It made sense to him. But from the moment Yufan's plan was implemented, teamwork turned to strife as each gull shifted focus to the self-centered goal of maintaining his or her place in the food court. The entire flock became increasingly aggressive in the pursuit of their next meal, which created a chaos that engulfed the food court. Patrons were dive-bombed on all sides by pecking gulls the moment their orders came sliding through the service windows. Food went flying, children left crying, and park employees scratched their heads over this abrupt change in the seagulls' behavior.

The park staff couldn't stand there scratching for long. They weren't about to have their customers scared away by a bunch of birds, and they decided that they must treat the gulls just the way a forest ranger treats a bear that has developed a taste for human food and won't stay away from campers. They would capture and relocate the aggressive seagulls.

As intelligent and swift as Scott was, his brazenness made him a primary target for capture. In fact, he was the only gull the humans came away with in their net, because their "hunt" sent the rest of the flock back to the roost in a panic. Kamikaze assaults on the food court ceased.

Charlie was off on the other side of the park when Scott was captured. When he returned to roost that evening, Maya and Yufan were waiting to speak to him.

"Bad news. Charlie." Yufan spoke first. "My plan didn't work so well, and the people captured Scott."

"Oh my!" Charlie was shocked and genuinely upset. "Where did they take him?"

"One of the dolphins overheard the humans saying something about taking Scott to the Salton Sea, way out there in the desert," Maya replied. "Poor thing; it's going to be a long flight home."

"What did he do to slip up and get captured?" Charlie asked.

"He was just doing what we all were doing, Charlie. We were fighting over the food because none of us wanted to be sent back to the seashore." Yufan said.

"I see," Charlie continued. "Looks like you guys are going to have to stop doing that."

"Oh, we're stopping, Charlie. We're going to go right back to what we were doing before all this. We're not going to change a thing," Maya said.

"Great! It's settled then," Charlie said happily.

"Not quite, Charlie. I'm sure you remember a few weeks ago when we all spoke to you. You said you'd change your approach. And you didn't," Yufan said.

Charlie gulped.

It was Charlie's job to manage the flock. He had promised to work alongside them and make things better. He had promised to change. Now the gulls were stuck— they were trapped in the food court and starved by the seagull manager that had led them there.

"We're through waiting around for you to change," Yufan continued. "There are a few new eggs that are ready to hatch into chicks, so we're going to have to stick around here for a month or so until they're out of the nest and can fly on their own. After that, we're returning to the seashore."

"You're *what?*" Charlie bellowed.

"We're leaving, Charlie. We've had enough of this," Yufan said.

"Maya, are you in on this?" Charlie asked.

"We all are, Charlie. It's been a long time coming," she said sadly.

Charlie looked up at the stoic faces surrounding him, and the room started to spin. For a gull who prided himself on his work, this was an intolerable position to be in.

"Don't be too hard on yourself, Charlie," Yufan said, placing a compassionate wing on his manager's shoulder. "It just didn't work out."

"It was fun while it lasted," Maya added.

Charlie reeled away from the other gulls, spun around, and flew off sulking. As the night wore on, competing thoughts tore through his brain. Since taking over the flock, all he'd ever done was try to help. He'd given years of blood, sweat, and tears to ensure their dominance over the food court. But now the old ways of doing things weren't working. Nothing seemed to be clicking, and Charlie didn't know why.

Midnight came and went, leaving Charlie deep in thought. He wanted to return to the roost with a plan. He wanted to prove to the flock that they could stay in the food court and be well taken care of. Most of all, he wanted to lead. He paced along the rim of the sea turtle tank until he was startled by a baritone voice that echoed from the darkness. Rattled by the sound, Charlie turned so abruptly that he slipped and fell backward into the water.

Charlie recovered quickly, using his webbed orange feet to right himself, and skimmed about the tank, peering into the darkness for the source of the interruption.

"Who's there?" he asked.

"I'm right here," a voice replied. This time the voice was so close that it sent Charlie flopping about again.

Charlie looked down and saw the scarred shell of an

old sea turtle floating beside him. The turtle's head poked high above the water's surface with a wry smile.

"Why did you scare me like that?" Charlie asked defensively.

"Oh, I'm sorry," the turtle replied. "I didn't mean to scare you."

"Then what are you bothering me for?" Charlie spat. "Can't you see I'm busy? I'm trying to think over here."

"Well," the turtle explained, "you looked like you could use some help."

"That's for sure," Charlie muttered under his breath.

"Indeed it is," the turtle answered back.

Charlie was instantly peeved. *Who does this guy think he is, a psychic? Imagine this sleepy old water dweller helping me. Boy, I'd looove to see that.*

"So, what is it exactly that I need help with?" he asked.

"My name is Oscar, for your information. And you, Charlie, need to come up with something quick if you're going to stay in charge of that flock of yours."

"Tell me something I don't already know!"

Oscar had captured Charlie's interest, hidden beneath the sarcasm. Charlie studied the turtle for a moment. He'd never paid much attention to the sea turtles in spite of their exhibit's proximity to the food court. Charlie was so busy each day that he'd hardly glanced in the direction of the turtle pool, let alone stopped by to say hello to his neighbors.

"So you've been watching me," Charlie said wryly.

"Indeed I have. And I must admit, Charlie, you're kind of hard to miss. You're always moving about, flapping your wings in the air, and squawking up a storm every time the other gulls get into a bind. It's really quite a scene," Oscar said.

"Thanks a million for those encouraging words, Oscar," Charlie said sarcastically, "but I'll be going now. I have to come up with a plan before morning, or you won't have a chance to see me *squawking up a storm* anymore." Charlie used his wings to contemptuously punctuate Oscar's words with imaginary quotation marks.

"Really? Why is that?" Oscar asked.

"You really want to know?" Charlie hesitated, realizing that he was about to spill his guts to a slow, flightless sea turtle.

"Absolutely. Fire away," Oscar said.

"Well, OK, here's the deal. You see, the flock is starving because the food court has become extremely competitive now that there are so many of us. Everybody says that I just make things worse when I try to solve their problems. But dang it, if I see some gulls in trouble, I'll be damned if I'm not going to go in there and lend a hand," Charlie said.

"That's admirable, Charlie, to care so much about your work and the gulls that work for you," Oscar observed. "So what do you suppose the flock wants you to do?"

"They want me to stop being me, I guess," Charlie moaned. "Either that or they want me to make food rain down from heaven."

"But why do you say they want you to stop being you?"

"I'm not really sure. I know there are things I do that frustrate everyone, but now it seems, with times as tight as they are, that it's taking everyone over the edge."

"*You're* taking them over the edge," Oscar stated.

"Well, I don't know about that," Charlie said defensively.

"Seems to me you're outnumbered in terms of who wants who to change."

"Well, I'll give you that one," Charlie replied as he stared off into space. He was beginning to fret again about what he was going to do with the flock.

"So, what's the plan?" Oscar asked.

"Mine? I don't have one. The gulls said they're gonna stick around for another month or so until the new chicks grow up a bit and then they're outta here. They're all heading back to live along the seashore."

"That's a shame."

Charlie nodded quietly, a wilted look of defeat on his face.

"Well, at least you have a month to do something about it," Oscar observed.

"Hardly. They've already made up their mind. Nothing I do is going to change their mind."

"Really?"

"Yes, really," Charlie snapped back. He was feeling a bit fired up again and he figured it must be because Oscar was being such a moron.

"What would you say if I told you that I have something you can take back to your flock that will regain their trust and get them to stay when the month is over?" Oscar asked.

"I'd say you're crazy," Charlie said, "unless maybe it's a warehouse filled with food."

"Nope, don't have that. I have something that will feed your flock much longer than a warehouse filled with food. In fact, it'll feed your flock forever—or as long as you're willing to *water the garden,* so to speak."

As annoying as he found Oscar's beating around the bush, Charlie couldn't deny that his suggestion was intriguing. "And what, exactly, do you have for me there, *turtle?*"

"I'm glad you asked. What I have is the only way you can expect to win back the support of your flock. You'll need to adopt the three virtues of superior managers."

Charlie threw his wings across his belly and acted as if he was going to throw up. "Oh, Gawd! Which anointed one decided that there are three virtues that will make *me* a better manager? Was it you, swimming around in this think tank of yours?"

Oscar couldn't help but laugh, "No, Charlie, I had to learn them myself before I could appreciate how important they are. I learned them from some friends of mine—friends who live outside of this pool." Oscar continued: "You see, I used to be something of a 'seagull manager' myself. I suppose I still am on rare occasions, but back then I was having many of the same troubles here in the pool that I've seen you having with your flock. Then I learned the three virtues, and they flip-flopped my approach to running this tank."

Charlie remained skeptical but, to his own surprise, felt compelled to ask, "And what are these three virtues of yours, turtle?"

"They're things that you—well anyone, really—needs to do as a manager," Oscar said. "And the only reason you aren't doing them now is that you aren't aware of them."

Oscar finally had Charlie's undivided attention.

"The first virtue is creating full-fledged expectations for every member of your flock. The second is altering your communication style, so that it clicks. And the final virtue is my personal favorite, though I have to admit it was the hardest for me to learn: paws on performance. All you need to do is learn 'em and use 'em, Charlie. They'll take care of the rest." Lost in his own excitement, Oscar had said a mouthful. He looked up and saw a blank look on Charlie's face.

Charlie cleared his throat, and the fire returned to his eyes. "Well, that's a nice little intellectual exercise you've got going here in your turtle pool, but let me tell you something—it ain't gonna fly in the real world.

In the real world we have to compete for our food. We don't just get to swim around all day conjuring up cockamamie theories while we wait for the attendants to come and feed us." Charlie was furiously. He exited the water and paced along the edge of the tank as he spoke. "I'm out of here! I can't believe I've wasted this much time already."

Oscar reached a flipper up over the pool's edge in front of Charlie, as if to stop him. "All right, Charlie, but before you go, let me ask you one question," he said calmly.

Charlie threw his wings on his hips and tapped a webbed foot impatiently while he waited for Oscar to speak.

"Would you be willing to learn the three virtues of great managers if I can prove to you that they do work in the real world?" Oscar asked.

Charlie remained there thinking for a moment. He knew he was out of options, though he doubted this old turtle had half a clue what he was talking about.

"What do you have to lose?" Oscar asked.

Charlie's wings fell to his side, and his foot stopped tapping, "All right, if you prove it, then I'll try and learn one of your virtues. But don't waste my time, turtle! I've got a lot of gulls relying on me."

"Great! You won't be disappointed. Tomorrow morning I want you to go meet a friend of mine. She's going to show you how the first of the three virtues works in the real world. Once she convinces you of that, she'll show you how to use it," Oscar said.

"Who's your friend, and where am I supposed to meet her?" Charlie asked.

"Her name is Imata. She's a sea otter. Just meet her over at the Otter Encounter exhibit."

"A sea otter? You can't be serious." Charlie's worried look quickly faded; for once, he had realized that his fretting was not about the otter. "Tell me, turtle, what's the point of this plan of yours to show me the three virtues of great managers? Why do you care whether I change?"

Oscar was slow to respond. "I suppose there are a couple of reasons. First off, your flock provides daily entertainment for us here in the pool. As you can imagine, it gets pretty boring for us swimming around and around in a circle all day when we used to be free to roam the ocean. Anyway, it's pure comedy watching your flock dive-bomb the humans to steal their food. We'd hate to see you all go."

"And the second reason?" Charlie asked with a wry smile.

"I wouldn't mind helping you, Charlie. You seem like a good guy, now that I've had the chance to get to know you a bit. And you're really in a tight spot here with the flock. I honestly believe that using the three virtues will get you back on their good side. *Permanently.*"

Charlie was silent.

"Look, you're just going to have to trust me, buddy—it's the only way I can help you," said Oscar. "Just head over to Otter Encounter first thing in the morning, and you'll see what I mean. Imata will be expecting you." And with that, Oscar drifted down deep into the murky water, leaving Charlie alone to choose his fate.

Chapter

3

Full-Fledged Expectations

CHARLIE TOOK OFF FOR THE Otter Encounter exhibit as soon as the sun came up. The air he floated on felt crisp and cool, which soothed his aching body. Stress and sleep deprivation had done a number on him in recent weeks, but he was determined to give this a try—even if it meant trusting the advice of a sea turtle.

Charlie wasn't quite sure why Oscar wanted him to go see the sea otters. He entered their rocky enclosure, looked around the tranquil pool, and saw a bunch of otters floating on their backs. They all seemed to be sleeping.

Great, he thought. *Oscar sends me here to watch a bunch of sea otters sleep. This is going to do wonders for me.*

Then Charlie noticed a pair of otters—one large and one small—swimming together. The little one climbed

up on top of the other, stretched out, and took a nap on her stomach. As the larger otter lay there floating lazily on her back, she noticed Charlie through a cracked eyelid, smiled, and waved him over with her paw. Charlie flew over and landed on the rock beside her.

"You must be Charlie," the otter said warmly. "Oscar told me you'd be stopping by this morning. My name is Imata. It's so nice to meet you."

"Good morning," Charlie said flatly. "Who's the leech?"

"Oh, him?" Imata smiled as she stroked the fur on the little otter's snout. "This is my boy Acha."

"You let him just hang on you like that?" Charlie asked.

"Sure I do." Imata gave Charlie a puzzled look. "What exactly do you mean?"

"I mean, he's a big boy. Looks to me like he should've been shoved out of the nest a long time ago."

"Oh, I see why you might think that. But I stay with a pup for a good six months before he can live on his own."

"What in Sam Hill do you give yourself all that extra work for?"

"It's the only way I can ensure he'll know what will be expected of him when he's on his own. Being a sea otter is not as easy as it looks, Charlie. We have to groom ourselves constantly and in just the right way to keep our coats working properly. We have to steer clear of killer whales and great white sharks. And I'd like to see you dive to the bottom of the ocean to fetch a sea urchin, let alone crack it open and eat it while you're swimming."

"Touché," Charlie said with an approving nod. Then he blurted out, "But you could show him how to be a dolphin, a penguin, *and* a sea otter in six months!"

"Touché yourself, Charlie," Imata said with a wry smile, "but you're missing the point. I could probably teach him how to be a dozen animals in six months, but I only want him to be one thing—a sea otter who knows how to handle himself."

"But why would you spend so much time doing that?"

"Because there's a big difference between telling or even showing someone what is expected of them and actually rolling up your sleeves to make sure they completely understand what they'll be expected to do in the future."

Imata saw that she had piqued Charlie's interest enough to go in for the kill, "That's why you're here, actually—to learn how to set Full-Fledged Expectations with your flock."

Charlie twitched his beak. "That doesn't make any sense. My gulls know what's expected of them. Get food and eat it. Period."

"You see, that's your problem. You can't manage anyone, or anything really, with vague goals. Telling your flock to 'go find food and eat it' and then waiting to see if they do it isn't managing at all."

"It isn't?"

"No, it isn't."

Charlie noticed a strange rumble in his belly. It wasn't hunger, and it didn't feel good.

"To manage is to achieve results by making use of what you have available to you. If you aren't setting crystal-clear expectations with every member of your flock, you won't see results. You're holding them back."

"But isn't food the expectation?" Charlie asked. "I *expect* them to get food."

"*No,*" Imata said, mimicking Charlie's tone. "Food is the result. It's the outcome."

"How's that?"

"What they do to get the food—that's the expectation. Think of it this way: you're not going to expect them to get food every time they try, are you?"

"No, that wouldn't be fair," Charlie said.

"But you *are* going to expect them to go after food as much as possible, aren't you?"

"Without a doubt," Charlie said.

"Hence, you have an expectation: you expect them to engage in the pursuit of food. And why do—"

"Because that's their job," Charlie said.

"Exactly. Now, let me ask you something. Have you ever shown the gulls how to go about getting food?" Imata asked without even a hint of irony on her face.

"Aw, come on now . . . they're seagulls, for crying out loud! If there's one thing we know how to do, it's how to eat," Charlie began pacing across the rock as he spoke.

"Oh *really*? Then why is your flock going hungry?" Imata asked.

Charlie stopped pacing. For once, he was speechless.

"Hey look, Charlie, you're not the only one who has something to learn about managing a group. But I've got a point to make that you need to hear, and I'm not going to let you sidestep it."

Charlie's stare slowly morphed into a slight, albeit approving, nod. Imata figured this was his way of saying that he was ready to listen.

"If you set Full-Fledged Expectations with a gull who joins your flock—or a member of your flock who's taking on a new role—it's inevitable that some of the discussions will revolve around things that that gull already knows how to do. And that's OK. If a gull proves to you that he already knows how to complete a particular task, you don't have to spend any time teaching it. You just move on to the next thing. Really, setting Full-Fledged Expectations isn't all about teaching—" Imata caught herself moving at an otter's pace, so she paused for a moment to make sure that Charlie was tracking. He was. He even smiled a little. *Smart bird,* she thought.

Imata continued: "It's not all about teaching, because your primary objective is making sure that the gull understands—in no uncertain terms—what you'll be expecting him or her to do in the future. The devil is in the details. If you get in there and think about the little things—talk to the gull about what it takes to do his job day in and day out—you pave the way for success. Invest your time in setting Full-Fledged Expectations for each bird, and the entire flock will take flight. That's a promise."

"What you're saying makes sense, but I need to get moving on this. I mean—when I leave here, how do I get right into setting Full-Fledged Expectations with my flock?" Charlie asked.

Imata was relieved to see him speaking again. "Pick a gull to start with. It's probably best if you begin with the one who needs the most help," she told him.

Imata helped Acha open a clam while Charlie tried to picture the skinniest gull in the flock. "Got one?" she asked.

"Ya, I . . ." Charlie stammered. "Hold on . . . lemme think . . . just another . . . got it! It's Alfred. Definitely Alfred. I don't know what his problem is, but he's the skinniest of the bunch—looks a lot like a squirt bottle."

Imata couldn't help but chuckle, "OK, great. Now picture Alfred doing his job *well*. What does that look like?"

"I don't know. He doesn't do his job well; that's why he's a toothpick."

"I suppose his job is locating food and consuming it?" Imata asked.

"And sharing some with the others if he's having a good day," Charlie answered.

"All right, but let's focus on square one," the otter continued. "Describe for me what it would look like if Alfred did a good job of getting hold of some food."

Charlie took an admiring look at his own bulging, rotund belly. "Oh, that's easy; he'd just do what I do," he said. Then he leaned toward Imata as if he were sharing a secret. "I like to call it Charlie's Paired Ps of Scoring Food." He punctuated the statement with a self-absorbed wink.

Charlie's self-esteem was finally getting a little push. If there was one thing he knew how to do, it was nab some grub in the food court, and he was thrilled to share. "It's a simple two-step system that ensures I can get food in any situation. Step 1 is Peruse."

"Peruse . . ." Imata echoed sarcastically. "Very fancy."

Now Charlie was the one on the spot, but he was too busy teaching to appreciate the irony. "Perusing the food court is the path of least resistance. You'd be surprised by the goodies you can find when you're cruising around the food court—leftovers on the tables, in the trash cans, all over. Plus, when I'm walking around the tables looking for food, some of the humans will even feed me."

"Maybe they think you're cute?" Imata asked with a grin. "What's the second P?"

"If I can't find enough food perusing, it's time to plunder. This one takes a little skill, but as long as you're aggressive, it can be done."

"Plunder?"

"You know, snatching churros from people, scaring a little kid away from a slice of pizza . . . Heck, I can dive in and pluck a hot dog out of a bun before a *Homo sapiens* even knows what hit him. Plundering is hard work, but it's a sure way to fill my belly when food is getting hard to come by."

This gull is too much, Imata thought with a slight chuckle. *Where did Oscar find this guy?*

"Whatever tickles your tummy, I guess. Seriously though, Charlie, you have something really great going on here that you can take back to your flock."

"Really?" Charlie asked, his eyes the size of dimes. It had been a long while since he'd felt the soothing tingle of praise.

"Without question. You have an escalating set of expectations that you can teach to any gull to ensure that he or she can get results. How many members of the flock have you taught your Ps to?" Imata asked.

"Um, let's see . . ." Charlie's beak tweaked a bit to the left, and his gaze fixed somewhere off in the distance. "There's Maya, Yufan, and, ummm . . . errr . . ." he gave a nervous glance over at Imata. It was obvious she was expecting more than two.

Charlie looked away and continued with a frown, "It's just those two."

"And how many gulls do you think would stand to gain from Charlie's Paired Ps of Scoring Food if you took the time to teach them?"

"Every single one of them," Charlie said with a grin. "Even the two I've already shown them to—Maya and Yufan—wouldn't mind a tune-up, I bet."

"I have to agree with you, Charlie. I know that any gull in your flock will benefit from your taking the time to set Full-Fledged Expectations for their work. You'll be handing them the keys to success. It's hard to fail when you know exactly what needs to be done *and* you know exactly how to do it."

"So that's why setting Full-Fledged Expectations is so—" Charlie rubbed the underside of his beak pensively as he spoke, and then he held a wing up toward Imata, "Could you hold on for just a second?"

"Sure," she replied.

Charlie took off from the rock and went hunting for a scrap of paper. He spotted a piece of napkin tumbling about in the wind, swooped down, and snatched it up in his beak. Charlie returned to his rocky perch above Imata and retrieved a stub of pencil that was lurking somewhere deep within his chest feathers. Then he spread the napkin out on the rock and furiously scribbled himself a note:

> ## YOU HAVE TO REVEAL EXACTLY WHAT NEEDS TO BE DONE BEFORE YOU CAN EXPECT TO TO SEE IT HAPPEN!!

Imata was so transfixed by this sequence that she failed to notice her pup was getting playful and ended up dunking her head under water. She resurfaced, shook her head like a wet dog, and resettled comfortably on her back. By this time Charlie was stuffing the pencil and the folded note back somewhere deep into his chest feathers.

"You keep a *pencil* in there?"

"Yup! You'd be surprised what I can squeeze in here."

Imata was certain there'd be more surprises in store if she were to get a good look at the knick-knacks hidden beneath Charlie's layers of down. She was also certain that she had *zero* interest in doing so. Thankfully, Charlie shifted the subject.

"I like to keep the pencil around so I can write myself a note from time to time. Notes get my attention long after I write them because I'm not used to carrying them around. It'll poke me or something, and I'll dig in there to see what it is and . . . voila! I'm reading the reminder I wrote to myself."

"Not a bad system, Charlie," Imata said with a nod of approval.

Meanwhile, her playful pup persisted with his frolics. The morning was wearing on, and he was used to mom's providing more engaging activities. There was grooming to learn, diving to practice, and shellfish to hunt and crack.

His impatience finally getting the better of him, Acha jumped off his mother's stomach and into the water. This sudden act of independence captured Charlie's attention. Watching Acha swim around on his own left Charlie puzzled.

"Imata?" Charlie asked, his gaze still fixed on the swimming youngster.

"Yes, Charlie."

"What do you do when he gets big? I mean, he's already husky for a little guy. You can't go carrying him around forever."

"Oh, he's big enough that I don't let him lie on me all day. He knows that I expect him to swim around on his own and build his strength. Nowadays, I don't even have to ask him to get started most of the time. He just does it."

"That's pretty cool," Charlie said happily. He was relieved to know that he wouldn't be spending the rest of his days walking his flock through their own jobs. "But what about when it's time to let him go? You can't just pull the plug on him, can you?"

"Well, I don't just shove him off into the wild, if that's what you're asking. From day one he's known that we're taking small, incremental steps toward his goal of living on his own. By the time the big day arrives, he'll be excited to go and prove himself. He'll be ready—they always are." Imata chuckled. Acha had just surfaced with a nice clam between his paws and a big grin on his face.

"How do *you* know they're ready to do it on their own?" Charlie asked.

"You just gradually increase your distance. Not always physical distance as much as giving them the space to complete tasks on their own. Let them fail a little until they learn how to get it right," Imata continued. "As long as you are near enough to observe their progress, guide the process, and offer a few pointers here and there, you'll know when they're ready to do it on their own."

Imata helped Acha finish prying open his clam and then continued, "You know, Acha is a pretty good example of this. Soon he'll be big enough and strong enough to swim and float without my help. When he gets there, I won't let him rest on my stomach anymore, but I still have ways of keeping him near until he's fully developed."

"What are we gonna' do, Momma?" Acha asked in his squeaky little voice.

"Well, honey, soon you're going to be strong enough that you can swim and float on your own, like Momma does. When you can do that, we'll float on our backs right next to each other, and I'll hold your paw to make sure you don't get pulled away from me by the currents. That way you can practice your floating and we'll still be together."

"That must be quite a sight—the two of you floating around linked at the paw," Charlie said with a smile.

"It's somethin', all right. Doesn't last long, though. When a pup gets to that point, he's *this close* to doing it all on his own," Imata smiled back. She gave Charlie a moment's pause to think about that one.

"The other day my trainers were chatting about some tourist that posted a video of me and my last pup holding paws onto something called YouTube. Said more than ten million humans have watched it."

"Humans are amused by the strangest things," Charlie commented, shaking his head.

"Tell me about it."

"I guess that's how to keep from micromanaging," Charlie conjectured. "At some point we must let them go and do their jobs."

"Who knew you were so good at managing?" Imata said with a wink. "Now that you know what's expected of *you* as a manager, there's only one thing left for you to do to make sure your flock's expectations are full fledged."

"What is it?" Charlie asked eagerly.

Squawk!

"Go and get started," Imata said, kicking herself into a backstroke with her pup, Acha, in tow. "You're ready, Charlie!" She yelled enthusiastically across the tank, pumping her little paw into the air. "Don't worry, just go for it!" Charlie watched for a moment as the otters drifted away from him and back into their own little world. There was nothing more to analyze—it was time for some action.

Back at the Helm

Charlie returned from the Otter Encounter just as the flock was gathering for their afternoon break. A bleary-eyed Scott was among them, having just completed the long flight back from the Salton Sea. As the break hour drew to a close, Scott took a seat next to Charlie. "Hey, Charlie," he said with a tired smile.

"Oh hey, Scott. How was your flight?" Charlie asked.

"Looong."

"Yup, that's quite a trek, that one," Charlie said before turning toward Scott and looking him in the eye. "Listen, I'm sorry that that happened to you. Doesn't seem right . . . those humans hauling you off like that."

"Live and learn, I guess." Scott shrugged. "Where were you this morning? I didn't see you when I landed."

"Uh, I had some things to take care of . . ." Charlie stammered a bit before realizing what he wanted to say. "You know—some adjustments and what have you. Gotta be prepared for all these changes coming up."

"Ya, I know. They told me about heading back to the seashore." Scott looked down and dragged his foot back and forth along the ground as he spoke. "Listen. Charlie, I'm real sorry that it's come to this. We've had some great times here, but now . . . now we're starving. We just don't have any other choice."

"I'm trying my best to accept that," Charlie said. "It seems to me that all of us are still after the same thing—right? Staying fed?"

Scott nodded.

"Well, I'm going to do everything I can with the time I've got left. If you all are stuck here another month, there's no sense in spending it starving."

"Good luck with that, boss. I know everyone will appreciate it if you can scare up some more food."

When the flock returned to the food court for the afternoon shift, Charlie got right into setting Full-Fledged Expectations. Just as Imata had suggested, he began with Alfred. Rail thin, with eyes that looked massive through the lenses of his Coke-bottle glasses, Alfred was an unassuming, shy, but eager student. He hung on Charlie's every word as the boss took him through Charlie's Paired Ps of Scoring Food.

"That's it, buddy. That's all there is to it! If you think you're ready, I'd like to test you out a bit before I cut you loose. You know, make sure that you've got it all down and you'll be all right on your own."

"Mmm . . . OK," Alfred said in his high-pitched, nasal voice.

Charlie watched eagerly as Alfred tried his hand at the first P. Alfred was polite and quiet as he moseyed about the food court, and the park patrons found him adorable. Food was thrown to him left and right, and Alfred snatched it up and took it back to Charlie.

"Not bad—*slick*—but let's see how you do when times get tough. I want to see you plunder!" Charlie said, pushing Alfred off of the retaining wall and back into the mix of tables.

Alfred continued his quiet pacing around the tables, ignoring the food landing at his feet, until he spotted what he wanted. He stopped and watched carefully as a guy with a bad fake tan, wearing a tight T-shirt, finished paying for his ice cream. The moment the beefcake stepped away from the window, Alfred flew toward him like a bat out of hell and snatched away his ice cream. In a flash he was back, setting the ice cream cone at the feet of a flabbergasted Charlie, and he did it all without spilling a drop.

"Look at this guy . . . he's an animal!" Charlie yelled, pointing at Alfred and searching frantically for an audience to this incredible transformation. Always the one to break his wing patting himself on the back, Charlie decided his work with Alfred was done right then and there.

He told Alfred to get to work on his own, and Charlie spent the rest of the week teaching the Ps to the rest of the flock. As he worked with the other gulls Charlie was surprised to find that most were already using the Ps in some capacity—though each gull had his or her own name for them. Even though some of the discussions were rehash, most every gull picked up something useful from this unexpected powwow with their boss.

Charlie knew Scott was the fattest and most skilled member of the flock, so he decided to work with his star gull last, figuring it would be a snap to ensure that expectations were full fledged. When the two gulls met after the close of the food court on Friday, Charlie found things to be just as he expected—Scott was great at locating food and had an excellent, intuitive understanding of the expectations for his job.

After fifteen minutes of touching base, Charlie figured his work was done. He suggested they call it a night, but Scott had other plans.

"Charlie?" Scott asked.

"Ya, buddy."

"I'd like to know what you think about something. The more time passes with the flock still starving, the more I've come to see it as an access problem. Even if every gull in the flock follows your Paired Ps perfectly, I still don't think there will be enough food to go around. There are more of us than mealtime at the food court can provide for. Look at it this way: I'm really great at snagging food—I can get my beak on way more food than I need—so I share it with everybody else. But we're still a flock of hungry gulls pecking at an inadequate food supply."

"It's great that you're so good at it—"

"That's it exactly. I'm so good enough at landing that it gets boring. I could use a new challenge," Scott explained. "Not to mention, it feels like I'm not really doing my job when I know that the others are still going hungry."

"I see . . ." Charlie began to realize that he was dead wrong—setting Full-Fledged Expectations with his star gull wasn't going to be easy or quick. "What is it you want to do with your time?"

"Well, remember the night shift idea I shared with you a while back? Before I got dumped out in the desert, I stayed up late a few nights and scouted the delivery schedules. I'm convinced that it will create a new food supply for the flock."

"It's a compelling idea, but what if it fails?"

"Then I'll explore other new alternatives that might expand our food supply. Not full time, of course," Scott said. "I don't even think the night shift should remove me from the bulk of my current responsibilities. I just need some room to prospect."

Charlie thought deeply about Scott's request He saw real sense in the suggestion that a gull could have unique expectations for his job that were tailored to his particular skill set and motivational needs. With a mental image of Imata letting her little pup go to sea to make his own way, Charlie decided to embrace Scott's plan.

"All right, then. Why don't we give this new idea of yours a whirl?" said Charlie. He looked directly at Scott, who was beaming, and fed off his excitement, "We'll make the process of exploration a new expectation for your job. Since every solution you pursue might not produce food, the expectation won't be that everything you try gets results. I'll just expect you to spend a third of your time trying hard to find new, creative ways to feed this flock."

Charlie's wholehearted support made Scott comfortable enough to show a little vulnerability, "What if none of my ideas work?"

"Hmmm . . ." Charlie said. He felt a growing sense that his work setting Full-Fledged Expectations for his flock was not complete. He decided to pay a visit to the turtle later for some advice.

"To be honest, I'm not sure," Charlie said, mirroring Scott's candor. "But I tell you what: I'll figure it out before we get there. For now, let's work on getting you started, 'cause we have a lot of starving gulls to feed."

The two spent the better part of the next three hours mapping out Scott's new role within the flock. Charlie told him everything he knew about running a night shift, they created counter-strategies to work around potential complications in Scott's plan, and Charlie was careful to outline exactly what he expected from Scott in his new role. Charlie even created a new title for Scott that signified his change in duties: Assistant Seagull Manager.

By the end of their extended meeting, the two gulls were exhausted, but there was also something festive about their situation—they were pursuing something new and different that left them feeling excited and more productive.

"You know, it's been a long day and an even longer week. What do you say we go blow off some steam?" Charlie asked.

"Really?" Scott asked.

"Oh, absolutely! Go grab Maya, Yufan, and anyone else who's in the mood, and we'll head over to the parking lot. I know where one of the attendants stashed a six-pack," the seagull manager said with a grin. "We'll poop on the cars, too."

"OK, sounds like a blast. I'll be right back."

As Charlie watched Scott head off to get the others, he was comforted by the realization that this was the first time in a long time when he felt happy at work.

Full-Fledged Expectations

~~❧~~

Ensure that employees' efforts are spent doing the right things the right way. This means thoroughly exploring what will be required of the employees, how their performance will be evaluated in the future, and getting agreement and commitment to work toward established goals. There is a big difference between telling people what's expected of them and making sure that what they'll be doing is completely understood.

Chapter

4

Communication That Clicks

LATE THAT SAME EVENING, WHEN Charlie returned
to roost after horsing around with Scott, Maya, and Yufan,
he stopped by the turtle pool to see if Oscar was up. Oscar
was awake and eager to hear how Charlie's week of setting
Full-Fledged Expectations with the flock had gone.

While the impact was noticeable, Charlie was concerned that his efforts weren't bearing enough fruit. "It's
just a lot of talking, and planning, and goal-setting," he
told Oscar, "but I know what they really want to see is
results. The whole point of me changing is to get them
fed, and other than the new food Scott's night crew is
bringing in, nothing's happening."

"Nothing?" Oscar probed.

"Well, not exactly *nothing*, but nowhere near what I
was hoping for. I know they could be getting fatter than

this in a week's time, so setting Full-Fledged Expectations isn't doing its job. It's not enough."

"I see," the turtle responded in his stoic baritone.

Half talking, half brainstorming, Charlie continued, "Take Alfred, for example. I thought he was a total geek until this week. He's so frail—he probably couldn't even fly away with a hot dog if there were too many condiments on it. So, I take him aside and show him all of my best techniques for scoring food, and he's a natural. I mean it, Oscar. You should've seen it—he shocked me he was so good at it. Snatching food left and right."

Charlie looked over at the turtle, who didn't seem surprised by Alfred's transformation.

"Anyway, a week has gone by now, and Alfred's hardly gained an ounce. I just don't get it . . ." Charlie trailed off.

"Think of it like you're building them a house, Charlie. At the very beginning of the construction, you can do one of two things: level the ground properly and lay a solid concrete foundation, or go right into building the structure. Building a solid foundation takes time, and at the end of the day it doesn't look like much, but the dwelling that rests on that foundation will stand the test of time."

"So you're saying that setting Full-Fledged Expectations is just the foundation?" the gull asked.

"Exactly. It doesn't tend to look like much when you're finished."

This perked Charlie up a little. "All right, I better get to the lumberyard, then. I've only got three more weeks to get this baby built."

"Good. Tomorrow I want you to head over to the dolphin petting pool. The dolphins will help you to get where you're going."

"The dolphins—are you sure?" Charlie sounded concerned. "Um, I kinda have a bad rap with the crew in the petting pool."

"Have I failed you yet, Charlie?" the turtle asked.

Charlie shook his head.

"Then you're just going to have to trust me again on this one. Don't worry about it now. You need to get some rest. You'll have to get there early tomorrow so you can take care of business before the park opens."

"Gotcha," Charlie said, with a wing pointed out at Oscar like a pistol. Charlie had been burned before, so trust didn't come easily these days. He was dead tired from a busy week, though, so he figured the best thing he could do was go and get some sleep. At least things might look a little brighter when he was fresh again in the morning.

A Date with the Dolphins

The next morning, broad beams of sunlight penetrated Charlie's eyelids to rouse him from slumber. He rubbed his eyes with his wings and took a look around. Though it was still early, it was already warm, and Charlie didn't see a cloud in the sky. This meant he'd better hurry—the park would be packed with people the moment it opened, and he was already losing valuable time with the dolphins. Before taking off for the petting pool, Charlie surveyed the sleeping gulls around him. They did look a little fatter through his rested eyes, but there was still a lot of work to be done.

Charlie hesitated high above the dolphin pool. The large mammals circling the tank below him looked antsy, and this made Charlie nervous. Like the sea turtles, the dolphins lived in a pool, but the dolphin pool was known around the park as the petting pool because tourists bought fish that they could use to lure the dolphins to the edge of the tank for a pat on the head or a rub of the snout. Given his skill at dive-bombing for food, Charlie couldn't resist swooping in on the unsuspecting tourists to snag their fish. Stealing the fish was a breeze when the humans were distracted by an oncoming dolphin, and Charlie was certain that the dolphins didn't appreciate him stealing meals out from under their noses.

Charlie dreaded confrontation with anything big enough to make a snack out of him. Even though dolphins don't eat seagulls, he imagined all sorts of horrible ways the intelligent creatures could pay him back for eating their food.

Have I failed you yet? Charlie reminded himself what

Oscar had said to him the night before and repeated it over and over again on the way down to the dolphins. He landed on the edge of the tank and was quickly over-whelmed by the swirling cauldron of fins, flippers, and blowholes that moved about before him. Feeling threat-ened, Charlie instinctively threw his wings back, puffed his chest out, and broke into a nervous strut along the edge of the tank.

As Charlie did an about-face and turned his strut in the opposite direction, the head of a bottle-nosed dolphin surfaced like a silent submarine in the water beside him. Charlie swaggered, and the dolphin followed, convincing the gull the moment he saw it that he was being preyed upon. Charlie went into attack mode, turned abruptly, and unleashed a machine-gun–like flurry of pecks on the end of the dolphin's snout. The dolphin just sat there un-til Charlie wore himself out from pecking.

The dolphin watched with a broad smile as Charlie pulled back from his attack and struggled to catch his breath. "Whew, doggie! That's some way to greet a new friend," the dolphin chuckled.

"I, ummm . . . aaa. . . ." Charlie had no idea what to say.

"Come on, buddy, relax! I'm just messing with ya," said the dolphin, laughing loudly. Then he calmed down, just a little. "I'm Hui, and *you* must be the C-man?"

Hui was the kind of dolphin that could sell ice cubes to penguins if he had to. What some attributed to a natural flair for social interaction, Hui knew was just a simple focus on whomever he was talking to first, instead of just thinking about himself. Hui liked to read what others were feeling and use this knowledge to guide his responses to them. Meeting Charlie, Hui spotted right away that this was a gull with a serious need to lighten up, and he wasn't afraid to act the fool to make it happen.

"Most people call me Charlie, but you can call me C-man if you want to, I guess," Charlie replied. *This dude is a burrito short of a combo plate,* he thought.

"Well then, C-man, I'm glad you stopped by," Hui continued. "We have a boatload of things to talk about."

Silence.

"What's wrong, C-man? Why so quiet?" Hui asked, undeterred by Charlie's standoffishness.

"Oh, nothing, I've just had a lot on my mind lately and—" Charlie stopped himself and took a deep breath. "I'm lying."

Hui threw him a confused look.

"I'm just kind of uncomfortable being here, given our history and all."

Charlie looked up at Hui to find that, like a statue, he hadn't changed. The look of confusion remained on his face.

"You don't know what I'm talking about?" Charlie asked in disbelief.

"Nope." The dolphin responded. "Not yet, anyway."

"The fish?" Charlie asked, expecting the light bulb to turn on for Hui.

"What fish?"

"You know . . . *the* fish—*your* fish. I've been stealing your fish!"

"Oooh, *those* fish . . ." Hui continued. "Ya, don't even worry about that. We don't care."

"You mean you don't enjoy the fish the humans feed you?" Charlie asked, confused.

"Aw, come on, man! No way! We *looove* those tasty li'l critters."

"What!? How come you aren't mad at me for taking them?"

"We were at first. I mean, when you guys showed up it was a bit of a shocker. All of the sudden there's this flock of seagulls that's living in the food court and snatching up everything they can get their beaks on. We'd never had anything like that here before." Hui continued, "We realized we had to adjust, ya know? What are we gonna do? Climb out of this pool late at night, slither on over to the food court, and eat ya?" Hui said with a deep belly laugh. "So, we developed a system to work around you guys snatching some of our fish."

"How's that?" Charlie asked.

"Well, have you ever noticed how when the people are feeding a dolphin he doesn't stick around for long?"

Charlie cocked his head to one side, looked straight down at Hui, and said, "Yes, I've always wondered about that, 'cause it doesn't add up. You guys don't strike me as the type to pass up an easy meal."

"True story, C-man, but they pack a lot of us into this tank, so we take turns to keep everybody fed. That's why a dolphin is splitsville once he gets a fish—we have a rotation. And that's how we deal with you when you steal a fish—we just adjust the rotation."

"Is that what you're going to teach me—to take turns?" Charlie asked. This sent the dolphin into another bout of deep guttural laughter, which he punctuated by spraying Charlie with a mouthful of water.

"Imata told me you were a card!" Hui chuckled.

"If I'm not here to—" Charlie said shaking himself dry. "Wait a minute! How do you know I met with Imata last week? Your exhibits aren't anywhere near each other."

"C-man . . ." Hui said, realizing that this gull had a lot to learn, "the pigeons deliver our messages for us."

"Seriously?"

"Dead serious, man. The pigeons ferry our messages around the park for us in exchange for fish."

"*Pigeons eat fish?*" Charlie asked with a gasp.

"Pigeons will eat *anything*, man."

"Well! You learn something new every day!" Charlie exclaimed.

"You'd be surprised what you dig up when you keep in touch, C-man. You know, some of your seagulls have been transmitting messages for us lately, too."

"No, they don't. Not my flock," Charlie said with conviction. "If they were seagulls from my flock I would know about it."

"You mean Maya and Yufan aren't in your flock anymore?" Hui asked. The dolphin knew exactly where he was taking this.

"Maya and Yufan are transmitting messages for you *for fish?*" Charlie spat. He was shocked and felt betrayed by this discovery.

"Only at night when they can no longer steal them from the tourists. They share 'em with the rest of the flock. Said the gulls were having a hard time finding enough food, so they had to put in some extra hours," Hui explained.

"That's not such a bad idea," said Charlie reluctantly, shaking his head. "But I can't believe nobody told me."

Charlie fell silent and just stood there above the dolphin, trying to absorb this bizarre series of discoveries in the dolphin tank.

"Oh, sorry, Hui. I was lost in thought there for a moment. What were you saying?"

"No worries, but we need to get crackin'—park opens in less than an hour. I was just saying that you'd be surprised at the stuff that comes up when you stay in touch with your flock."

"But I *do* stay in touch. I talk to them every day," Charlie said. "Like when I come in, in the morning . . .

I'll say hi to everybody, crack some jokes, you know, stuff like that."

"Do you talk to them about how their work is going?" Hui asked.

"How their work is going . . ." Charlie said under his breath, repeating Hui. Once Charlie had thoroughly considered the question, he looked up and said, "Not as much as I'd like to, at any rate. It's hard!"

"What makes it hard?"

"Well, time for one. There's only one of me to go around, and every time I get locked in a discussion with a gull it pulls me away from my duties. And there are a lot of gulls in my flock. Some days I'll have three, four, five—who knows *how many* of them—that want to discuss something important. I don't think there are enough hours in the day for me to stay connected with everyone."

"And the other reason?"

"Most of my conversations with members of the flock aren't very productive. Everyone has their own ideas for why we should do *this*, or they wonder why we don't do *that*. Even during the good times, when everyone was really happy with how things were going, the conversations were always about things that could be done differently. I'm a man of action, and these conversations just bog me down."

"And that's why you don't communicate as much as you should?" Hui asked.

"Something like that . . ."

"You're an easy one to fix, then, C-man!" Hui said encouragingly.

"I am?" the confused seagull asked.

"Well, *yaaa*. Your only problem is you're approaching your job the wrong way. Think about it. Your job title is *manager*. Your sole purpose is to help them perform. Isn't it?"

"Now that you mention it."

"Your only concern should be your flock's performance, and I gotta tell you somethin', C-man. I don't care if they're seagulls, dolphins, or those humans lining up at the gate right now to get into the park—we *all* rely on the manager we report to. We need our manager's support and our manager's guidance, and we certainly have to defer to our manager's authority. If your manager doesn't listen to your ideas, then who will?"

"You have a point there, Hui. But I wouldn't give the humans that much credit if I were you," Charlie said with a devious grin.

"Awww, come on now!" Hui laughed. "Just because we've trained them to come here and pay money so they can feed us doesn't mean they don't have the same feelings and thoughts that we do."

The two watched for a moment as one of the park employees who was cleaning the pavement chased another employee around with the hose.

"You have to maintain a constant flow of communication with all members of your flock if you want them to be successful. You're the glue that holds everything to-gether, and you're not doing a thing if you aren't opening that beak of yours."

"Can you hold on a quick second?" Charlie asked, reaching toward his chest and poking around for his pencil stub. Hui waited patiently while Charlie scribbled himself a note.

IF YOU AREN'T STAYING IN TOUCH YOU AREN'T DOING YOUR JOB!!

"Like I was saying, C-man, communication clicks when it's constant. You, my feathered friend, are at the other end of the scale. You don't communicate with your flock all that much because you don't even realize what your job is really about."

"I guess I don't."

"You're gettin' distracted by the laundry list of *stuff* you have to do each day, when your top priority should be communicating with your team," Hui said. "Your job is eating you alive because you're running away from it. You're like a gardener who's upset because the darn grass keeps growing."

"Well, when you say it that way . . ." Charlie pondered.

"You've been setting expectations with your flock since you saw Imata, right?" Hui asked.

"Yep."

"Have you noticed how, once an expectation is set, it feels like the job isn't quite done?"

"Yes, I have! I've also noticed that setting expectations didn't fatten the gulls up that much."

"Well, C-man, you're not alone. You need to take the next step with your flock and get your communication clicking if you want to see results. Just make it a priority. Stay in touch with everybody so you can monitor their progress, help them solve tough problems, and just let them know that you have their back," Hui explained.

"Because I'm their manager, and that's what they need from me the most."

"You got it, bud!" Hui exclaimed with an excited splash. "Hey, listen—they just opened the front gates, so I gotta bounce. I have a pod of my own here that I need to get in touch with if we're gonna have a good day raking in the fish. You get on back to your flock and get communicating with them. All you need to remember is to keep the flow of communication steady if you want it to click. And once it does click? Watch out, C-man! You're gonna have a lot of chunky seagulls around!"

As he watched Hui flop back toward the middle of the tank, Charlie contorted his wing tip into a makeshift hang-loose sign to let his surfer-dude teacher know that everything would be all right. But deep down, Charlie wasn't so sure. *Here I go again,* he thought, and he took off for the food court once more to try his hand at something new.

Communication That Clicks

Back at the food court, Charlie decided to start where he had finished the prior evening. He found Scott and asked him how things were going with the night shift plans. To the seagull manager's surprise, Scott and his crew had already run their first shift the previous evening. Scott told him that their mission had borne fruit, and the rest of the flock was happy to have breakfast for a change before heading out for a hard day's work in the food court. Scott's audacity in beginning the night shift mere hours after he'd been given the green light reminded Charlie just how hungry his flock was. As soon as he could tell that Scott was satisfied with their check-in, Charlie headed straight for Alfred.

Charlie landed on the planter adjacent to the dining tables and spotted Alfred strolling along at the tourists' feet. The park-goers threw food Alfred's way by the hand-ful, just as they had the week prior. Every ounce of Char-lie's being told him to swoop in there and set that skinny gull straight, but the more he thought about it, the more he realized he'd only be blasting the poor nerd with hot air. Alfred had no problems getting food; yet, he was as skinny as ever, and Charlie had no idea why. So, instead of swooping in on the gull, as he would have just weeks before, the seagull manager watched and waited.

Charlie's patience was soon rewarded. He watched as Alfred gathered the food into small piles he had hidden under a bush. He flew laps around the tables time and time again, collecting as much food as his scrawny frame could carry. When the lunch hour had passed and the humans had dispersed into other areas of the park, Alfred called the other gulls over and had them eat *his* food! Like a bunch of trained pigeons, the flock gulped down Al-fred's food until scarcely a crumb was left on the ground. It took the flock only five minutes to eat all the food, and, as much as Alfred had collected, it was just a drop in the bucket of the flock's daily dietary needs.

Alfred smiled as the seagulls took off and went back to what they were doing, and he began stockpiling food all over again. For once, Charlie had waited long enough to spot the right moment.

"Hey, Al, how's it going?" Charlie asked.

"Good," Alfred replied.

Charlie stopped for a moment once he realized that this was the first time in months he'd heard Alfred. It also happened to be the first time Charlie had asked him a question. "I've noticed you're pretty skinny, and I wonder if I can help?"

"OK."

Charlie scratched his head. It sure was easier to make communication click when he was talking to Scott. Charlie cleared his throat. "Is there anything I can help you with?"

"You want to help me collect food?" Alfred asked.

"Ummm . . . I'd be happy to," Charlie sighed. As he walked around the tables with Alfred—who continued to have food rained upon him while the humans scarcely threw Charlie a crumb—he felt like a failure. *Here I am supposed to be helping this guy eat, and all I'm doing is helping him collect food*, Charlie thought.

Just when Charlie was feeling the weight of the temptation to fly away or yell at Alfred to get his droppings together, a pigeon landed next to Charlie and started talking.

"Hey, yous. Who heah is Chalie?" the city pigeon asked.

"I'm Charlie—and what's it to you?"

"I got a message for ya," the pigeon said. Then he dropped a piece of paper at Charlie's feet and took off.

Charlie uncrumpled the paper and read it:

Squawk!

Hey, C-man,
You dropped this in the pool.
Peace,
 Hui

A second piece of paper, which looked strangely familiar, fell out of Hui's note and landed at Charlie's feet. Charlie shook his head as he read this serendipitous note-to-himself, "IF YOU AREN'T STAYING IN TOUCH, YOU AREN'T DOING YOUR JOB." *All right,* he thought, *that rules out flying away, but what am I going to do with this guy?*

As Charlie moved to throw Hui's note away he noticed more writing on the back:

P.S.
Give it time, C-man. Staying in touch isn't a
means to an end. It is the end.

Charlie heeded Hui's advice and allowed himself to focus all of attention on communicating with Alfred. As he helped Alfred transfer the food into piles under a bush, Charlie struggled to find something useful to say. And then it hit him. "Al," Charlie queried, "why do you collect all this food to give away to the rest of the flock?"

"Because I like them and they are starving," Alfred said, his voice coming out of his nostrils as much as his mouth.

That tiny little sentence contained more words than Charlie had ever heard from this gull, and it was all he needed to hear. Charlie was relieved to finally discover the source of Alfred's problems, and he felt a rush of gratitude for having this bona fide team player in his flock. Dealing with a bleeding heart was going to be so much easier than the nightmare scenarios Charlie had imagined.

"Buddy," Charlie continued, "you are good at collecting food. I take that back. You're downright incredible at it!" Charlie smiled boisterously and draped a wing around Alfred's shoulders. "But you need to feed yourself, too. Feeding yourself is your job, and it's crucial . . ." Charlie paused to think, and he could see that Alfred was listening closely. "You've probably noticed that even with all the food you collect, it's never enough to feed the whole flock?"

Alfred nodded his head.

"I'd like you to fill your belly first, and once you're stuffed you can go and collect food for the others. Is that all right with you?"

"Yes," Alfred said with a smile.

"All right, then. That's what I'll be evaluating— how much fatter you're getting. And try not to worry too much about the others; I'll be spending a lot of time with them to make sure they're finding ways to get enough food."

When he returned to roost that evening, Charlie

was tempted to send Hui a thank-you note for saving the situation with Alfred. Instead, he decided to be more open-minded in embracing the dolphin's touchy-feely approach to communication; Charlie figured this was the most heartfelt thank-you he could provide.

Communication
That Clicks

—⁓—

*Observe what employees say and
do, and speak openly with them
about their work. A manager's
interaction with his or her
employees delivers the resources,
guidance, and recognition they
need to succeed. Communication
clicks when it is frequent and
in a language that everyone
understands.*

Chapter

5

Paws on Performance

As THE WEEKS BUZZED BY, Charlie noticed that the hatchlings, who seemed only yesterday to still have egg fragments in their down, were up and out of the nest. He could read the writing on the wall—it wouldn't be long before the flock moved back to the seashore. This troubled Charlie greatly. He didn't want to lose his flock under any circumstances, and the progress he'd made over the past month made the thought of their exit even more difficult to bear. Charlie had worked hard to narrow his focus sharply on the quality of his communication with the flock. He had learned a ton about each gull in the process, and the conversations they shared unearthed a plethora of new, more effective ways to get work done.

That's not to say that making communication click came easily for Charlie. He had old habits to shake, a new schedule to manage, and previous misconceptions about what it meant to be a manager that wouldn't just disappear. The seagull manager found himself caught in a juggling act between his desire to always be *doing something* and the flock's need to just have him around. The only straightforward part for Charlie was that his communication with the flock was contagious. The more he stayed in touch and maintained steady contact with each flock member, the more they all came to rely on it. Communication became the habit that held the flock together.

As efficient and aligned as the flock had become, there were still a few gulls who hadn't fattened up much. Charlie yearned to know what more he could do to feed his entire flock, convince them all to stay, or at least win back their trust, and he knew just where to go to find out.

When Charlie arrived at the turtle pool, he found Oscar in his usual element—the pool was pitch black, and a mysterious haze rose from the water's surface before dissipating into the cool night air. No longer a stranger to the unknown, Charlie plopped fearlessly into the water and began searching for his shelled friend.

Oscar spotted the outline of a plump shorebird bobbing about above him and figured that it must be Charlie. The old turtle surfaced and said, "Hey, pal, long time no see."

"There you are. Can't they put some lights in this thing?" Charlie asked, exasperated. "Listen, I need your help with something."

"You know I'm all ears," Oscar replied.

"The chicks are getting *big,* man. It's making me nervous."

"I guess it was only a matter of time," the turtle waxed philosophic. Charlie bristled, so Oscar shifted gears. "Are you having any luck getting your communication to click?"

"Yes, actually, I am. That's why it's taken me so long to get back here to learn that last virtue. What's it called again?" Charlie asked.

"Paws on Performance."

"Right, boss. I don't mean to rush you, but it's already been a month since they announced the mutiny, and they'll be heading back to the seashore any day now. I need to learn the last virtue *fast* so that they can see that I'm a changed bird." Charlie waved his wings about frantically as he spoke.

"How does tomorrow morning sound? I'm sure I can get Annabel to see you then."

"Can't you just tell me about it now?"

"I could tell you about it, but I won't be able to teach you what you need to know," the turtle explained.

"Well, why not?"

"For one, I'm not a canine," Oscar continued, "and, like you did with the first two virtues, you'll need to experience Paws on Performance in order to make it your own. You'll get that over at the Super Pets Show tomorrow."

"So Paws on Performance will get my flock to stay?"

"No, not exactly," Oscar said, leaving the seagull visibly disappointed.

"Then what's the point of learning Paws on Performance if it's not going to keep my flock from returning to the seashore?" Charlie huffed.

"There's an old Chinese proverb that says *Give a man a fish and you feed him for a day. Teach a man to fish and you feed him for a lifetime.* Tomorrow you'll take it one step further—you'll learn how to ensure a lifetime of abundance."

Once again, Charlie found the turtle hard to argue with, so he thanked him for setting up the meeting and returned to the roost to get some rest.

Managing Performance Like a Super Pet

Charlie was munching on breakfast early the following morning when he noticed the flock had removed the nests that housed the chicks. *They're really going through with it,* he thought. *What a great day this is going to be! Might as well have someone carry me over to the Super Pets on a platter so they can put me out of this misery.*

Charlie exited the roost and flew toward the Super Pets Show arena. It was his first visit there, and on any other day he would have been completely terrified. Charlie lived in an aquatic theme park for a reason—there was safety in having the predators confined to the water. The Super Pets Show was an anomaly. It was crawling with dogs, cats, and even birds that would jump at the chance to turn Charlie into a meal, but today Charlie was too worried about losing his flock to fret about being eaten.

As Charlie approached the arena he spotted a black-and-white border collie scanning the skies attentively from the main stage. The collie saw Charlie and waved him down with one of her front paws. "Charlie?" she asked as he landed on the stage beside her.

"Guilty as charged. You must be Annabel," Charlie replied, extending a wing in her direction for a shake.

"Why, you don't look a bit scared," Annabel observed with a thick Scots burr. "Oscar told me you'd be worrying about a sneak attack from a Labrador or something."

Charlie chuckled at the thought of the old turtle speaking so frankly about him. "Ya, I guess you could say that I'm not myself today."

"Because your flock is on its way out?"

"Yes. Any day now they'll be heading back to the seashore. Makes me wonder why I'm even still trying."

"Well, they're still here, *aren't they*?" Annabel raised her voice enough to rouse Charlie from surrender.

"I suppose they still are."

"Then what are we waiting for? I need to teach you Paws on Performance so you can take it back to that flock of yours and show them what you're capable of."

"All right."

"First thing you need to understand is why so many managers fail to manage their employees' performance successfully. Seems too many of us worry about being a *nice boss* or a *mean boss* when in truth a manager is neither of those things," Annabel said.

"I'm not?" Charlie asked.

"You're a mean boss, actually, but if you start doing your job correctly the gulls will stop seeing you that way. I'm sure Imata told you that your sole purpose as a manager is to guide your employees to results?" Annabel asked rhetorically. Charlie nodded his head in agreement. "Well, how can that happen if you aren't letting them know whether they're doing things the right way or the wrong way?"

"I always tell them when they're doing it wrong," Charlie said proudly.

"And that's why they think you're a mean boss."

"Oh."

"Problem is, you correct their mistakes only when it's convenient for you—flying in at the last minute to squawk at them, or letting them have it when they've really blown it."

"And I suppose the *nice* bosses come over and give everyone hugs and pats on the back when they're screwing up?" Charlie asked with a slight sneer.

"No, nice bosses also engage their employees only when it's convenient. Since praise is what they find convenient, nice bosses swoop in every time someone is doing something right. Nice bosses ignore mistakes just as often as you ignore triumphs."

Charlie was too busy processing this to conjure up a comeback.

"Most managers stick with praise because it's the fun and fulfilling part of guiding someone toward results. It feels good to let somebody know they're doing a great job. The toughest part of being a manager is *constructively* correcting employees when they're off track. But superior managers balance praise with constructive criticism because they understand their sole purpose—"

"Is to guide their employees to results," Charlie said triumphantly.

"I couldn't have said it better myself," Annabel responded with a wink.

"What you're suggesting—balancing the two—makes sense to me, but how do you find the time? I mean, it seems like I wouldn't have any day left once I'm through following everyone around to praise and correct them."

"Let me put it to you this way, Charlie." Annabel gave a penetrating stare as she spoke. "My breed are revered for our ability to keep things in place. Ranchers entrust us with their livelihood because they know we will keep the herd on track and en route to the desired destination. Do you know how we border collies go about that? How a single dog can keep an entire herd of sheep together?"

"Lots of biting?"

Charlie's attempt at humor fell flat as Annabel continued, "An errant member of the herd is not a failure; it's a signal that my help is needed. I approach these indiscretions eagerly because they give me an opportunity to do my job. I don't expect every ram and ewe to fall in line perfectly with every step, so I make sure I'm there to show them the way when they get off track. There's no need for biting when you take an assertive, yet nonthreatening, approach to mistakes. The herd responds to me because they know I'm not going to nip at their heels or chase them around aimlessly; they know I'm there to help them get back on track."

"You said that superior managers balance correcting mistakes with praise, but I don't see any praise in there," Charlie said bluntly.

"Well, my whole goal is to make my relationship with them a positive one. I find that if I'm around long enough to spot mistakes, I'm also there to catch them doing things right. Imagine an ewe that's right on track—she's leading the herd into an undulating ravine that I need them to traverse. I let her know it. I open my mouth and make her feel good. They need praise just as much as you or I do, so I approach it with the same energy and enthusiasm that I bring to correcting mistakes. In the end they don't fret about which angle I'm coming from because they know me as a supportive presence who is actively engaged in helping them achieve success."

"But how do you keep from micromanaging? Paws on Performance sounds an awful lot like I'll be sticking my beak in places that will drive my flock batty."

"I know what you mean. You aren't the only one who's afraid of being labeled a micromanager." Annabel paused for a moment to gauge Charlie's reaction to this statement. He had taken out a pencil and a paper napkin and was looking eagerly in her direction, so she continued, "But a lot of managers these days are so terrified of that moniker that they take the opposite approach. They lose touch with their staff, problems fester, and the team loses direction. Then they find themselves even more tempted to come in at the last minute and—"

"Squawk up a storm and poop all over everybody and everything. They become seagull managers!" Charlie pointed a wing skyward to punctuate the statement.

"Not quite how I was going to say it, but absolutely correct, nonetheless," Annabel said with a smile. "A manager's problems are much easier to handle when he tackles them while they are big enough to see, yet still small enough to solve. It's your job to stay connected with your team and involved in their work. Whether or not you twist that into micromanagement is a measure of your own insecurity, obsessive need for control, or what have you. If you practice Paws on Performance, your gulls can go about their work independently and without reservation, content in the knowledge that you will connect with them when your guidance is needed."

"Can you hold on for a second?" Charlie asked, picking up his pencil and the paper napkin.

"Sorry, Charlie; I can't. I have a show to get ready for. Take your time, though. None of the other actors will be out here for a good half hour."

"Oh, OK," said Charlie with a shrug. "Thanks for helping me."

"Any time, Charlie. You know just where to find me," Annabel said with a wink. She ran off backstage.

Suddenly alone, Charlie struggled to regain his train of thought. As he looked out at the empty arena he wondered if he'd even have a chance to get more help from Annabel, or if he'd just be a solitary gull with no flock of his own to manage. Charlie took hold of his pencil and sketched a reminder to use Paws on Performance.

PAWS ON PERFORMANCE ENSURES I:
✓ PRAISE WORK THAT'S WELL DONE
✓ GUIDE ERRANT PERFORMERS BACK ON TRACK
✓ GIVE THE FLOCK A HEALTHY SENSE OF INDEPENDENCE & INTERDEPENDENCE

MICRO MANAGER

SEAGULL MANAGER

Wings on Performance

As soon as Charlie finished writing, he took off for the food court. Soaring through the sky, Charlie couldn't help but ponder Annabel's teachings and Oscar's purpose in sending him to see her. It was obvious to Charlie that communication serves as the linchpin of good management. That comforted him, since he'd spent so much precious time learning it.

Charlie also realized that he needed to put Paws on Performance to work. Without it, all the effort he'd expended in setting Full-Fledged Expectations and establishing Communication That Clicks would fall to waste. For the first time, Charlie grasped the extent to which it was his duty as manager to roll up his sleeves and orchestrate the flock's performance. Suddenly, things looked as clear as the sunny San Diego skies he was floating on.

Charlie was thrilled to see the flock hard at work in the food court, and he jumped right into the mix. Alfred caught his attention first. The now portly gull was buzzing about the tables, stealing food from the tourists in a manic frenzy. Charlie chuckled to himself at the wisdom of Annabel's teachings. Here he was, just five minutes removed from their meeting, and his first opportunity to use Paws on Performance was staring him in the face.

"Hey, buddy, how's it going?" Charlie asked.

Alfred was standing above a tray of nachos drenched in cheese. He gulped down whole chips so ravenously

that Charlie could see each one wedge its way down his narrow esophagus. "Great!" Alfred beamed between swallows.

"No kidding! You're doing a great job feeding yourself. All this food you've been scoring has fattened you up nicely," Charlie said.

"Thanks," Alfred smiled.

"There's also something that I'd like you to do differently," Charlie said, and paused. Constructive criticism came so readily to him that he wanted to make sure Alfred felt nothing more than a mellow nudge in the right direction. "You see, plundering isn't your only strength. You're also great at perusing. And when you peruse, the humans throw you food voluntarily, which means it doesn't bother the park employees. Plundering, on the other hand, creates a scene that irritates the park staff. So I'd like you to save your plundering for those times when you aren't getting enough food from perusing. This way, the humans are less likely to want to boot us out of here."

"Ay, ay, captain!" Alfred said, throwing his wing against his forehead in a quirky, albeit earnest, salute.

As Charlie made the rounds with the rest of the flock that afternoon he followed Annabel's suggestions and balanced constructive criticism with frequent, genuine praise. When it came to Charlie's calls for improvement, most of the flock didn't even notice the difference, other than that their manager spent far less time nitpicking inconsequential mistakes. But the other half of the equation—the newly positive, encouraging, even enthusiastic Charlie—turned heads. It was unlike anything the flock had ever seen from him, and for many of the gulls it was the first time they had ever received a compliment from the seagull manager. Charlie's praise initiated a contagious confidence within the flock, and he was surprised by how deeply even simple compliments were felt.

Charlie's only problem now was time—he had spent every second the seagulls had given him. He saw nothing standing between his flock and a return to the seashore. As he settled in to roost, Charlie was plagued by a sense that the winds of change were stirring. Though he couldn't know it now, he'd awake the following morning to bear the full brunt of their force.

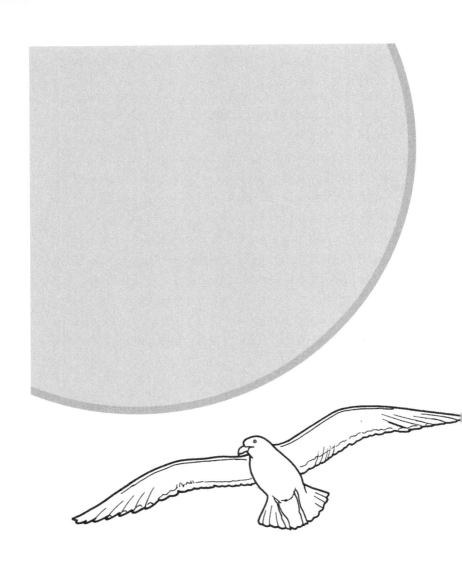

Paws on Performance

~~~

Pay attention to each employee's performance, and offer praise as frequently and emphatically as you do constructive feedback. Keeping your paws on performance pushes your team to new heights by positively reinforcing successful endeavors and realigning efforts that become misdirected.

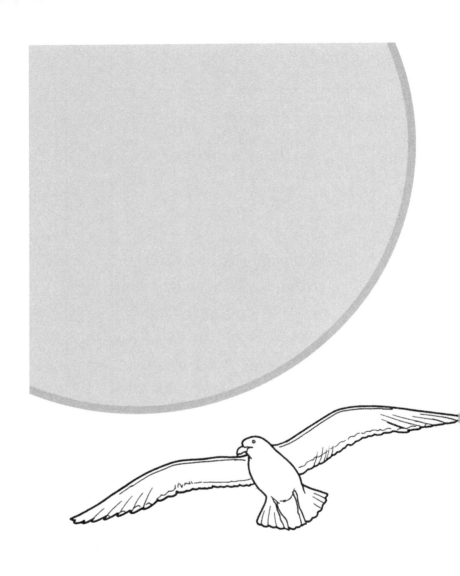

Chapter

6

A New Day

THE NEXT MORNING, CHARLIE AWOKE to an abrupt poke in the belly from a pigeon.

"Yo, Butterball! Wake up! I got an urgent message for ya," the brusque pigeon shouted.

Charlie rubbed the sleep from his eyes and recognized the pigeon as the same one that had delivered a message the day he'd met with Hui. Before Charlie could conjure up a clever reply, the pigeon fluttered off. A note lay in his stead.

Charlie unfolded the paper cautiously. It read:

> *Come see me ASAP.*
> *Oscar*

Squawk!

Charlie looked at the sleeping gulls resting peacefully beside him. The sun had yet to pierce the horizon. Standing there in the dim morning light, he was sad to think that their perches would soon lie empty. He dragged himself through the darkness to see Oscar. The unexpected snatch from slumber left Charlie's mind numb as he circled silently above the turtle pool. A full moon was still in the sky, and it cast a warming light upon the water's surface. A solitary, craggy turtle head was illuminated by the light's glow, and Charlie recognized it immediately as Oscar's.

Charlie landed on the edge of the tank alongside Oscar, who greeted him eagerly. "Hey, Charlie, thanks for coming over so quickly."

"No problem," Charlie said, his sleepy eyes still half shut.

"Well, I have some big news for you," Oscar said. The usually placid old turtle was bubbling with excitement, and it freaked Charlie out a little to see him this way. "The park wants to put your flock in a show!"

"A what?"

"A show. Your *own* show!"

"Aw, come on now. Quit pulling my chain," Charlie said. He wondered if sea turtles could get Alzheimer's. "I'm going back to bed."

"I couldn't be more serious about this, Charlie. They want to showcase some of your breed's unique abilities. They even have a name picked out—the Amazing Seagull Show."

"But why us?" Charlie asked perplexedly.

"Well, to be frank, the humans have been shocked by the changes they've seen in your flock over the course of the last month. The intelligence and resourcefulness your gulls are using to locate food amazes them. The seabird experts didn't even know your breed was capable of the things your gulls are doing."

"Aw, shucks." Charlie blushed. "What is it they want us to do?"

"Perform stunts that showcase your talents and wow the audience, just like they have the other animals do in their shows. They need only a handful of gulls to perform, but if the gulls agree to do the show, the humans will provide enough food for the entire flock."

"Which gulls do they want to perfor—" Charlie snapped his head back and forth as if he'd just been slapped. "What'd you just say? Did you say they'd give us enough food for the entire flock?"

"Yes, sir."

"This is it!" Charlie jumped up and threw his wings into the air. "This Amazing Seagull Show will get them to stay."

"I don't know about that," Oscar said with a shrug of his flippers. "You better go and speak to them."

"You're right, you're right," Charlie said as he paced the edge of the tank. He could scarcely contain his excitement and broke into a self-imposed lecture as he moved back and forth. "I need to communicate with them. I can't just make assumptions about their work. Let's see . . . let's see, oh!" Charlie turned toward Oscar. "Who is it they want in the show?"

"The only gull they're insisting on is Alfred. They think it'll be funny and cute to have him waddling around innocently making sneak attacks on the actors. They want Maya and Scott to showcase their intellect through a series of problem-solving games, and a few others to perform flying tricks. Oh, and they're also considering you for some precision-guided pooping—hitting targets and such from high above the arena."

"This is just too good to be true!" Charlie beamed. "You'll have to forgive me," he said as he spun around and took off in a frenzy for the roost, "I'm going to see if they'll stay!"

The Beginning in the End

Though the sun had barely crept above the horizon, Charlie felt wide awake. He rushed the roost in a manic burst that sent feathers flying in every direction. Charlie flew from gull to gull, jarring them awake and shouting, "Big news! Wake up! I've got big news!"

"*Charlie,*" Scott moaned, "What is all the fuss about?"

"Gather round, everybody. Come on, gather round." Charlie waved the flock in his direction, and one by one the sleepy gulls waddled over to him. "I just spoke to a friend of mine, and he shared some fantastic news about us. The park wants to do a show that features . . . *us!* An Amazing Seagull Show!"

"No way!" Maya yelled in excitement.

"Are you certain about this?" Scott asked.

"One hundred percent," Charlie explained. "They want Alfred to be the star, and a few more of us to perform in it. If we do it, they'll provide enough food for *the entire flock.*"

Cheers erupted from the group, as well as a flurry of wings as everyone vied for a chance to pat Alfred on the back. There were smiles all around as Charlie took the flock through the ins and outs of the park's plans for the Amazing Seagull Show. Like Charlie, the gulls were thrilled by the opportunity, and he hoped this enthusiasm would inspire them to stay. To Charlie's disappointment, the gulls gave no inkling that the show was going to keep them around.

"Listen, I've been noticing that the fledglings have, you know, been getting *big*," Charlie said. "We were roughhousing the other day, and the little buggers were flying circles around me."

"They're a healthy bunch, aren't they?" Maya asked, to nods of approval from everyone.

A grateful pause to reflect on the health of the flock's newest members stretched into an awkward silence for Charlie. "Look . . . I'll just come out with it," he stam-

mered, struggling to catch his rapidly increasing breath. "I know you were planning on leaving when the chicks made it out of the nest, but I wonder, with this new Amazing Seagull Show and all, if you guys might be willing to stay?"

Charlie's question spawned bewildered looks. Charlie gulped.

"Gee, Charlie," Scott responded sheepishly, "looks like we're better at keeping a secret than we thought."

"Secret? What secret?" Charlie asked nervously.

"That we've decided to stay." Maya's voice swelled with emotion. "Look, we're thrilled about the show, but that's not the reason we're sticking around. It's you, Charlie—we're staying because of *you*."

Charlie paused for a moment to collect himself. This discovery was so much to absorb that he just didn't know what to say.

Scott could see a flood of emotion welling up in the seagull manager's eyes, so he gave him a quick hug and a warm smile. "You changed so drastically that we didn't know what to make of it at first. We didn't know what puddle you'd been drinking from, but we didn't really care—it did the trick! We liked the new you, and we started trusting you again. We're confident now that you can lead us through thick and thin. We *want* to work for *you*."

"But the nests—" Charlie choked on suppressed tears. "Why did you tear down all the nests if you planned to stay?"

"We figure we should take it easy on growth until we're certain we've moved all the way through this rough patch," Scott explained. "We think you can manage an even bigger flock than we have now, but there's no sense in putting undue pressure on ourselves."

"Sounds like a plan!" Charlie gushed. "It sounds like a very smart plan."

Time proved just how smart the gulls' plan was. The Amazing Seagull Show was an instant sensation—the gulls' innate intelligence, resourcefulness, and hunting skills dazzled crowds at every performance—but it didn't entirely solve their food problems. To keep every belly full, the gulls still had to forage the food court and work together to discover new sources of food. They continued to rely on Charlie's leadership, and he relied on the three virtues of superior managers to keep the flock running like a well-oiled machine.

The gulls' bellies remained full, the nests returned, and the flock grew with each passing year. The flock expanded so profusely that Charlie realized it was time to let some of the more experienced gulls try managing a flock of their own. Charlie taught each new manager the three virtues of superior managers, and the new flocks branched out to inhabit new locations. Today, Charlie's seagulls are just about everywhere—amusement parks, sports stadiums, crowded cities, even Disneyland. Take a look around and you'll find them—healthy, happy, and plump. When you do see them, keep an eye out, or those chubby birds will steal your food faster than you think, and remember one very important thing about Charlie's seagulls—all their great achievements are possible because a single seagull manager opened his mind enough to let them spread their wings.

Part Two

~

The Model

Chapter

7

The Three Virtues of
Superior Managers

IN THE COURSE OF MY work with organizations
large and small, I've witnessed a peculiar commonality
among the most successful enterprises. These companies
step confidently beyond the success strategies of conventional business wisdom—brand strength, strategic leadership, technological innovation, customer service, and the
like—to leverage the single greatest resource inside every
company: its people.

Few organizations recognize the degree to which
managers are the vessels of a company's culture, and even
fewer work diligently, through training and coaching
programs, to ensure that their vessels hold the knowledge
and skills that motivate employees to perform, feel satisfied, and love their jobs.

Through my involvement in the TalentSmart Study—an effort to go inside the world's leading organizations and differentiate the habits that produce success from those that are inconsequential or harmful—I've obtained a bird's-eye view of the practices that are essential to a manager's job performance *and* the satisfaction of his or her staff.

To date, the TalentSmart Study has analyzed more than 150,000 managers in every industry, at every level of management, and in a wide variety of job functions, and we've found that superior managers—those who lead their teams to the greatest levels of performance and job satisfaction—often share three critical habits. These habits, or *virtues of superior managers*, as Charlie comes to know them in the story, are the polar opposites of the three distinguishing characteristics of a seagull manager: swooping, squawking, and dumping.

Whereas the seagull manager creates the need to swoop in and set his team straight, the superior manager gets everyone headed in the right direction from the very beginning by ensuring that expectations are full fledged. Whereas the rare visit from the seagull manager results in a lot of squawking, the superior manager maintains a steady flow of clear Communication That Clicks. And whereas the seagull manager manages his team's performance by dumping on everybody, the superior manager keeps his paws on performance—ensuring that positive and negative feedback are delivered in small, digestible doses.

Charlie's story illuminates simple truths that any manager can rely on to squash his or her seagull tendencies and transform the workplace:

Full-Fledged Expectations

Ensure that employees' efforts are spent doing the right things the right way. This means thoroughly exploring what will be required of the employees, how their performance will be evaluated in the future, and getting agreement and commitment to work toward established goals. There is a big difference between telling people what's expected of them and making sure that what they'll be doing is completely understood.

Communication That Clicks

Observe what employees say and do, and speak openly with them about their work. A manager's interaction with his or her employees delivers the resources, guidance, and recognition they need to succeed. Communication clicks when it is frequent and in a language that everyone understands.

Paws on Performance

Pay attention to each employee's performance, and offer praise as frequently and emphatically as you do constructive feedback. Keeping your paws on performance pushes your team to new heights by positively reinforcing successful endeavors and realigning efforts that become misdirected.

The three virtues of superior managers are intricately linked, with Communication That Clicks serving as the linchpin of the manager's efforts. In teaching these virtues to Charlie, Oscar and the other animal managers did more than give him new skills to use on the job; they reshaped Charlie's understanding of what his job really is.

Charlie realizes that his job is to support the members of his colony, not order them around, and that focusing on his role as supporter is the only way he'll be able to maintain the virtues of superior managers. Oscar watches with a silent smile as Charlie learns to set Full-Fledged Expectations, provide Communication That Clicks, and enable his flock's success through Paws on Performance. Charlie's transformation turns him from a highly problematic seagull manager into a tried-and-true superior manager who is tirelessly dedicated to the needs of his flock. Charlie's paradigm shift is so radical that it enables his flock to succeed in ways they—and everyone else—never thought possible, and this, for the first time in a very long time, makes Charlie thrilled to go to work.

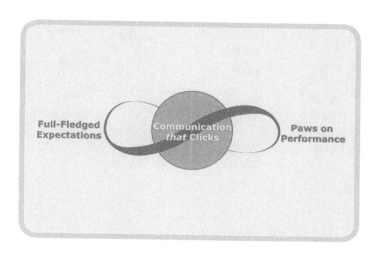

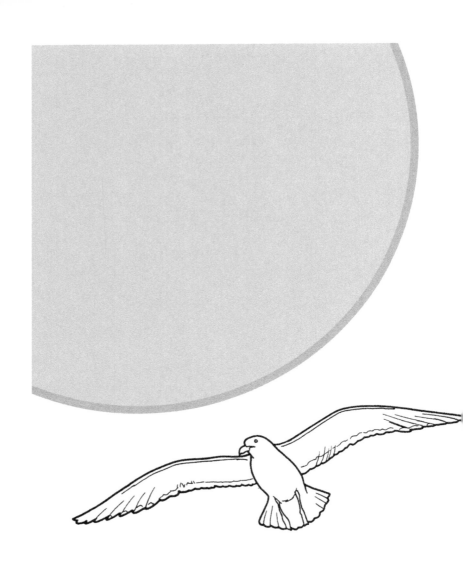

Chapter

8

The Cost of Seagull Management

PEOPLE MAY JOIN COMPANIES, BUT they will leave bosses. No one influences an employee's morale and productivity more than his or her supervisor. It's that simple. Yet, as common as this knowledge may seem, it clearly hasn't been enough to change the way that managers and organizations treat people. We've all been there—sitting in the shadow of a seagull manager who decided it was time to roll up his or her sleeves, swoop in, and squawk up a storm. Instead of taking the time to get the facts straight and work alongside the team to realize a viable solution, the seagull manager deposits steaming piles of formulaic advice and then abruptly takes off, leaving everyone else behind to clean up the mess. Seagull managers interact with their employees only when there's a fire to put out. Even then, they move in and out so hastily—and put so little thought into their approach—that they make bad situations worse by frustrating and alienating those who need them the most.

The seagull manager is an increasingly common phenomenon hovering in today's workplace. As companies flatten in response to the competitive changes created by new technology, industry regulation, and expanding global trade, they gut their management layers. The remaining managers are left with more autonomy, greater responsibility, and more people to manage. That means they have less time and less accountability for focusing on the primary purpose of their job—managing people. While there have probably always been seagull managers hovering inside the workplace, the recent flattening of organizations is breeding them like wildfire.

It's easy to spot a seagull manager when you're on the receiving end of their airborne dumps, but the manager doing the squawking is often unaware of the negative impact of this behavior. And they aren't the only ones. In the vast majority of organizations, senior leadership is unschooled in the profoundly negative impact the seagull managers hovering about their organization are having on its bottom line. The very individuals with the authority to alter the course of an organization's culture lack the facts that would impel them to do so.

Charlie's story may be fiction, but his tale is a characterization of some hard truths we have to face every day in the world of work:

> *Thirty-two percent of employees spend at least twenty hours per month complaining about their boss.[1]*
> *Employees whose manager often uses seagull-type behaviors are 30 percent more likely to develop coronary heart disease than employees of a manager who rarely uses these behaviors.[2]*
> *More than two thirds of North Americans are actively considering leaving their current job, with their employers suffering annual losses in excess of $360 billion from this employee dissatisfaction.[3]*
> *Approximately 50 percent of Americans hate their jobs,4 and job satisfaction has sunk to the lowest level in twenty years.[5]*

Some facts remind us that it's not easy being the one in charge:

> *Twenty-one percent of people would be willing to take their boss's job.[6]*
> *Thirty-five percent of employees have a tough time communicating with their boss.[7]*
> *Sixty-four percent of managers admit that they need to work on their management skills. When asked where they are supposed to focus, managers overwhelmingly say, "Bringing in the numbers"; yet, they are most often fired for poor people skills.[8]*
> *After more than twenty years satirizing management culture through his wildly successful Dilbert comic*

strip, Scott Adams agreed to roll up his sleeves and manage a restaurant he had co-owned for years from a safe distance. His foray into the rough-and-tumble world of management was a humbling one, and he was honest about his shortcomings in the real world, "I'm quite sure I've succumbed to. . . . flying in every so often and dumping on everything." There's a seagull manager born every minute!

Notes

1. From a study of 587 employees across various organizations by DDI, Inc., that was described by Mark McGraw, "Facts and Figures," *Human Resource Executive* (November 2005): 94.

2. From a study that followed 6,442 male employees for ten years. Seagull-type manager behaviors were significantly linked to incidence of coronary heart disease before and after the study, adjusted for conventional risk factors such as age, cholesterol level, body mass index, smoking habits, hypertension, alcohol consumption, physical inactivity, and other characteristics of the work environment. Mika Kivimaki, PhD, et al., "Justice at Work and Reduced Risk of Coronary Heart Disease Among Employees," *Archives of Internal Medicine,* 165, no. 19 (October 24, 2005): 2245–51.

3. From the large-scale Gallup Poll of the US workplace, available on line at http://www.gallup.com/poll/101905/Gallup-Poll.aspx.

4. Derived from a composite of the data in the following sources: data on a representative sample of 5,000 US households, conducted for the Conference Board, "U.S. Job Satisfaction Declines," February

23, 2007, available on line at www.conference-board.org/utilities/press; the large-scale Gallup Poll of the US workplace, available on line at http://www.gallup.com/poll/101905/Gallup-Poll.aspx; and responses from 14,095 MSNBC.com readers, available on line at www.msnbc.msn.com/id/17349102/.

5. From MSNBC.com, "Americans hate jobs more than ever," February 25, 2007, available on line at www.msnbc.msn.com/id/17348695/.

6. From a survey of 1,054 full-time male and female workers of all ages by the School of Business at the College of William & Mary in Williamsburg, Virginia, available on line at http://mason.wm.edu/Mason/News+Events/News/News+Archive/.

7. From ASTD (American Society of Training & Development), "Bad News Gets Easier," *T+D* (November 2005): 16.

8. From a summary of more than thirty-five years of research on 4,559 managers and 944 Human Resource representatives in forty-two countries by Paul R. Bernthal, et al. "Leadership Forecast 2005–2006," *DDI Executive Summary*, available on line at www.ddiworld.com.

9. From an article by Brad Stone, "The Tables Turn for Dilbert's Creator," *New York Times,* November 11, 2007.

9

Are You a Seagull Manager?

IF THIS BOOK HAS ACHIEVED its purpose, you've asked yourself that question at some point along the way. But the real question is not *are you* a seagull manager but *when are you* a seagull manager. It would be wonderfully simple—albeit frightening—if we could each be categorized as the "right" or "wrong" kind of manager. My biggest fear in writing this book is that it will be used to target "problem" managers, when the reality is that we're all the problem. That's right. Every single one of us is a seagull manager sometimes, in some situations, and with some people. The real challenge lies in understanding where your seagull tendencies get the better of you, so that you can fly higher and eradicate the negative influences of seagull behavior.

And the title of seagull manager isn't reserved

solely for those who manage others in a formal capacity. Whether you're an engineer, a professional skier, a homemaker, a seasoned manager in the traditional sense, or a novice climbing the corporate ladder, the key is to spot the situations where you engage in a seagull style of management of the problems you face. The key to overcoming seagull management is to tackle challenges when they are big enough to see, yet still small enough to solve. Your present challenges may include time management, stress, a personal relationship, your kids, your co-workers, or—as is often the case—all of the above! While it's impossible to make every action perfect, it's entirely possible to change your approach to problems, how you manage people, and, ultimately, how you manage yourself.

Printed in Great Britain
by Amazon

43075820R00078